Project Management
secrets

The experts tell all!

About the author

Matthew Batchelor MA, FRSA, MAPM is a member of the Association for Project Management (APM), and a judge of the association's annual achievement awards. He has over 20 years' experience managing publishing, design and marketing communications projects, and helping people in the voluntary, public and private sectors to deliver project programmes and high-impact communications.

Author's note

Many people have helped, either directly or indirectly, with compiling this book, including Iain Bain, Tim Holton, Brian Lawler, 'Beans' Hines, Robbie Steinhouse, Graham Woodward at APM, and Giles Barker. Thanks too to Gareth and Hilary, my parents Brian and Judy, wife Sarah, and children Ellen, Lucy and Joel.

Project Management
secrets

Collins
A division of HarperCollins*Publishers*
77-85 Fulham Palace Road, London W6 8JB

www.BusinessSecrets.net

First published in Great Britain in 2010 by HarperCollins*Publishers*
Published in Canada by HarperCollins*Canada*. www.harpercollins.ca
Published in Australia by HarperCollins*Australia*. www.harpercollins.com.au
Published in India by HarperCollins*PublishersIndia*. www.harpercollins.co.in

1

Copyright © HarperCollins*Publishers* 2010

Matthew Batchelor asserts the moral right to be identified as the author of this work.

A catalogue record for this book is available from the British Library.

ISBN 978-0-00-732810-9

Printed and bound at Clays Ltd, St Ives plc

Contents

Good project management is vital to business success

In today's highly competitive business world, more and more organizations are moving to a project approach. Whether launching a new, multi-million-dollar product or planning an office move, project management will enable you to deliver high-quality results on time and within budget.

Just as important, it provides a framework for continuous learning and improvement. In my own field of communications, I've spent over 20 years as a project manager, delivering projects as diverse as product launches and health conferences. I've observed a range of different project management approaches in action, and tried to adopt the best of them to improve the quality of the projects I manage.

Successful project management is about good systems and good leadership, to be sure, but it's also about exercising good judgement when required. This book will help you develop all three of these skills.

It aims to impart what I believe are the 50 most important project management **secrets** I've learnt along the way. These **secrets** are divided into seven key chapters:

Understand the role of projects. This section introduces you to the world of project management and helps you choose the right approach.
Aspire to succeed. To start your project you need a clear 'vision' and the ability to convince people to support your project.
Plan for success. Learn how to use Gantt charts, network diagrams and other essential tools for the project manager.
Manage your money. This section tells you how to build a project budget, manage risks and allocate contingency (extra); it will also help you identify the key areas to focus on to keep costs under control.
Lead and inspire your team. How to recruit, manage and fire up your project team.
Turn your plan into reality. Introduces some of the most common project management software, shows how to monitor progress accurately, and how to diagnose and solve problems.
Maximize project learning. Shows you how to close a project properly and conduct an effective evaluation.

Whether you are an experienced project manager or novice, if you follow these simple rules, you will be more confident in your ability to lead projects succesfully. This book will not only teach you how to act like a project manager but also enable you to think like one!

Great leadership, effective systems and making good judgements are vital in project management.

Understand the role of projects

This chapter aims to give you an understanding of the essential background to project management. It discusses the concept of the project life cycle, introduces the main stakeholders, and describes the role of the project manager. The most popular approaches to managing projects are discussed, along with some of the most popular software tools.

1.1

Projects are not tasks

Before getting started, it's worth understanding what a 'project' actually is. The UK Association of Project Management (APM) defines a project as 'a unique, transient endeavour undertaken to achieve a desired outcome'. In other words, a project has a defined beginning, middle and end, and a stated purpose.

Managing a project therefore differs from fulfilling a task, programme or professional work role. The following list helps to differentiate a project from other types of work.

■ **A project has a specified outcome.** Unlike a job or work role where you are likely to have aims that change over time, a project sets out to achieve a stated goal (or goals) within a certain timetable.

■ **A project involves a number of different tasks.** These tasks are generally defined as the smallest useful units of work. Related tasks are often combined into work packages or activities, which can be assigned to a single supplier or team.

■ **Each task will ideally be carried out by someone with suitable skills.** Project working therefore calls for a multidisciplinary approach. The more complex a project, the greater the degree to which people and tasks need to be carefully matched.

■ **A project is self-contained.** It has its own aims, timetable and resources. That's not to say that projects should be sealed off from the rest of the business – they can and should utilize skills and resources possessed by the wider organization, and the lessons learned should be exported to other colleagues and teams, and used on future projects.

Though they are capable of standing alone, projects may be linked to a wider programme of work, or be part of a portfolio of similar projects.

Adopting a project approach can yield significant benefits by defining clear outcomes against which to measure the input of resources and the quality of the project team and leadership. A project's resources can be human, or financial or physical – equipment and so on.

A project should have a clear time frame and be undertaken to achieve a desired outcome.

Understand project constraints

Planning your project will involve making a series of assumptions and a consideration of the constraints facing your project. Understanding these factors will help you plan a project that is of the right size and has appropriate objectives.

The assumptions you might make about a project normally involve things such as:

■ **Scope (scale).** How big is the project? Where does it fit into what your organization is doing? Roughly how much money is likely to be available?
■ **People.** Who can I get to help deliver this project?
■ **Physical resources.** What equipment and meeting space, for example, will be available?

None of this information has to be 100 per cent (or even 90 per cent) accurate at the outset. Nevertheless, understanding the assumptions around a project is an important first step – even if at this stage there are more questions than answers!

A useful way of looking at the constraints faced by projects is known as the 'project triangle'. This model describes three main things to consider for any project:

■ **Time.** How much of it do you have to complete your project?
■ **Cost.** What is the available budget?
■ **Quality (or specification).** Are you aiming to deliver something fairly basic, or more of a 'Rolls Royce' model?

With any project you will face a series of decisions about whereabouts in the triangle you position your project. For example, let's say you are asked to complete an office move for your company. If you are asked to complete the move over a weekend at short notice, and given only a limited budget, you are unlikely to be able to deliver the best results. So the costs and time used will be low, but so will the quality. If you are given more time, the results will be better; if you have more time and a bigger budget, they will be better still.

Another dimension often added to this diagram is people. For any given amount of time and money, the greater the skill and motivation of the people involved, the better the results will be. Looked at this way, the triangle becomes a pyramid, with the project manager leading his or her team upward to achieve the best possible results within a given schedule and budget.

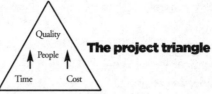

The project triangle

For your project, try listing the following in priority order – speed, quality and low cost.

1.3

Understand the project life cycle

All projects have a recognizable 'life cycle'. There are many different approaches to managing projects, but all agree that projects can be divided into various stages, each requiring a different focus.

The most straightforward life cycle approach recognizes four main stages of a project: aspiration, planning, implementation and measurement. You can easily memorize this life cycle because the stages both represent and substitute the words for how **A P**roject **I**s **M**anaged:

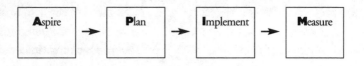

1   **Aspire** This stage focuses on the creation of a shared vision for your project. What are you aiming to achieve and why? How will you recognize and measure success? Whose support will you need to begin the project, and what will convince them to support you?

2 Plan This stage looks in detail at identifying what needs to be done to deliver your project successfully. What are the various tasks that need to be done, and how can they best fit together? Who will you need on your project team? What resources will you need, both financial and physical (equipment, meeting spaces and so on)? What are the main risks to successful delivery, and how can these be avoided (or at least minimized)? Lastly, how will the project be managed, and progress communicated?

3 Implement This stage can be divided into two parts: motivating and monitoring. At the beginning of your project you will need to form and motivate your project team, and agree the project's aims and working methods. Once your project is underway, your role shifts to monitoring – what progress has been made? What if any changes need to be made to the original plan? Is your project running on time, or has the schedule slipped? Are the costs as expected, or is the project in danger of going over budget? Have any problems been reported and discussed, and any necessary changes to the plan or budget been agreed?

4 Measure Once the project is complete, the final role of the project manager is to determine its success and to communicate the results, so that the lessons learned can be incorporated into other projects. To what extent were the original aims achieved? What went well and what went not so well? What lessons are there for future projects?

Adopting a life cycle approach will help you focus on the most important issues at each stage of the project.

1.4

Know your stakeholders

There are likely to be several different groups of people taking an interest in your project. Collectively, these people are known as 'stakeholders'. It's important to understand the actual stake each group has in the project – otherwise it may be difficult to balance what may seem like competing priorities. Here we outline the key roles.

■ **Sponsor.** The person who has asked you to undertake the project, and to whom you are accountable for its success. Often, this will be a senior manager within your organization – maybe your immediate boss. On larger projects, or within larger organizations, you may be asked to report to the sponsor via a project executive.

■ **Customers or users.** These are the people who will make use of the product or service you are designing, whether it be a new school, a product launch party or a company database. A key concern for this group is usability.

■ **Suppliers.** This group of stakeholders will undertake the design and delivery of your product or service, to ensure it meets the needs of users or customers. Suppliers also play an important part in risk management.

one minute wonder A useful way of classifying a project's stakeholders is by assessing how interested each group is in the outcome of your project, and the authority they have over it. This enables you to work out the best way to communicate with each group throughout the project, which is essential both in ensuring continued support and in planning your time.

	Low interest	High interest
Low authority	'Minimal effort'	'Keep informed'
High authority	'Keep satisfied'	'Key players'

■ **Project team.** The people who will help you deliver the project. These could be colleagues from within your existing team, others from across the organization, externally recruited specialists, or a mixture of all three.

■ **Project manager.** That's probably you! The project manager is accountable for the planning and delivery of the project, including progress reporting and project team management. Hopefully, one of the reasons you are reading this book is to discover more about this role, which we'll discuss in more detail in the next section.

■ **Others.** Depending on the nature of your project, other stakeholders might include your board of directors, the media, local or national politicians or industry regulators – even your competitors.

Take time to identify the main stakeholders for your project.

1.5

See your stakeholders' points of view

As project manager, your role is to understand the perspectives of individual stakeholders and bring them together into a shared vision for the project. This involves taking a 'helicopter view', to see the project as a whole.

■ **Business aims of the project.** The project sponsor is interested in the business aims of the project. 'What value will this project bring to the business?' and 'What is its role in our strategic development?' are likely questions he or she might ask.

case study Carole was asked to take on a project to upgrade her company's website. She started by asking each of the main stakeholders what they thought would constitute success for the project. The project sponsor, one of the company directors, replied: "I'd like you to deliver the project on time and within budget, and to keep everyone happy." The IT manager was less concerned with how the new site would work than with ensuring it would integrate well with the

■ **Benefits of the project.** The customer wants to know what benefits the project will bring to them and how they will be able to make use of the end product.

■ **Capability of the project.** The skills and resources of suppliers and the project team determine the project's capability. They will help you answer the question, "How can I successfully deliver what customers and users need, within the available schedule and budget?"

This diagram, adapted from the popular PRINCE2™ project approach (see page 23), shows how you can think about bringing these potentially diverse perspectives together.

Understand your stakeholders' perspectives, and bring them together in a shared vision for the project.

existing IT system. Other managers stated different priorities. The supplier said "Project, what project? All we've been given is a list of required modifications." Reflecting on these comments, Carol was concerned at the lack of clarity and shared understanding of the project. Her next step was very sensibly to call a meeting of all the main stakeholders, in order to define the key success factors and build a shared sense of purpose.

1.6

Choose the right approach

Modern project management emerged in the 1950s, with the development of a series of techniques aimed at making planning, estimating and controlling costs and schedules more effective.

You may not need to use a formal methodology for a small project, but it is still useful to know what the main methods are.

■ **The traditional, or 'waterfall' approach.** This approach treats projects as a straightforward series of steps from beginning to end. Each phase must be completed before the next begins. If, for example, your company is planning to upgrade its website, then all the user requirements must be known before the programmers begin work.

case study Ali worked for a recruitment agency, where she was asked to install a new database. She felt that the user requirements were not made clear and that the suggested timetable was possibly unrealistic. She decided to adopt an 'agile' approach to the project, where she and her team would meet twice a

■ **PRINCE2™.** This framework for managing projects was developed by the UK Government and IBM and is now used in more than 50 countries worldwide. It describes the different project roles and tasks, how to design and monitor a project, and what to do if the project isn't going according to plan.

■ **'Agile' or 'lightweight' project management.** This is a more informal approach based on breaking down tasks into small units, with minimal long-term planning. It is descended from the 'Lean' manufacturing approach pioneered by Toyota, and often uses a framework known as Scrum. Team sizes are kept small, with face-to-face communication preferred over lengthy written reports. Agility (flexibility) is the key.

■ **Critical chain (CCPM).** This aims to reduce project costs and timescales by making the best possible use of resources (people).

Other approaches stress the need for the close integration of project management and a wider business strategy, and emphasize the importance of becoming a learning organization.

A list of useful online resources appears in the further reading section at the end of this book.

Familiarize yourself with the main approaches to project management.

week at the start of the day to discuss problems and set short-term goals. They managed to install a working version of the new database by the specified launch date, using feedback from staff on this 'first release' to make modifications that were incorporated into the final version.

1.7

'The buck stops here'

Though everyone connected with the project has a role to play in bringing it to fruition, it is you, as project manager, who is ultimately responsible for its success. You are uniquely placed to see how the different elements fit together, and to drive your team forward towards completion.

Good project management rests on three fundamentals. It's about having the right systems in place, inspiring high performance through good leadership, and exercising sound judgement when required. These are some of the key things you need:

■ **Process selection.** It's important to use the right tools to cover all the areas of managing a project. Before you begin the project, you will need to decide how you are going to approach planning and scheduling, budgeting and resource planning, risk management, progress monitoring and communication, and evaluation. If this sounds like a long list, don't worry! All these aspects of project management are covered in this book.

■ **Approaches and methods.** You can choose from a number of different approaches to managing projects (Secret 1.6).

> **"Project managers function as band-leaders who pull together their players, each a specialist with an individual score"** L.R. Sayles, business writer

■ **Software to help you manage your project.** Software shouldn't be too cumbersome: ensure it is appropriate to the size of the project, otherwise you may find yourself working late every evening preparing plans and monitoring reports that nobody reads!

■ **Leadership skills.** In modern project management, leadership involves more than just managing your project team (essential though this is). It's about communicating effectively with all your stakeholders, to build and gain support for your project. In *Project Leadership*, Wendy Briner and colleagues describe how project leaders must manage the team, stakeholders and processes in order to be successful. (Project leadership is covered in Chapter 5.)

■ **Accurate, up-to-date information.** Juggling these priorities requires the ability to 'see the big picture', so that you can zoom in to where action is required. You'll need to ensure you have reliable information about the status of your project, so that you can use your judgement to make an informed decision – sometimes quickly. (There's more on this in Chapter 6.)

■ **Overview of the stakeholders.** From your 'control tower', take a little time to reflect on what other stakeholders are doing to help deliver your project, and what they expect from the project. How well do these expectations fit together? If there is a mismatch, these may need resolving – either by discussion (to agree priorities) or by amending the plan.

Juggling priorities requires the ability to see the big picture.

Many an 'old master' painting started with an initial rough drawing; colours were then added and lines redrawn to produce the final picture. In the same way, every project has to start somewhere – whether as a flash of inspiration in the bath tub, or a more structured solution to a strategic problem. It's important to know how to develop a project from these initial – and often rather vague – ideas into something more concrete.

2.1

Every masterpiece starts with a sketch

Projects don't grow on trees, nor emerge out of thin air. As more companies adopt a project approach, they are recognizing early on when a work area should become a project: a peak in business activity with defined beginning and end points, requiring a multi-disciplinary team to carry it out.

Recognizing, initiating and developing a project idea are essential skills for any aspiring project manager.

1 Like trees, projects need strong roots. Make sure your project idea is grounded in the needs of your business, or it will be unlikely to command much support. Similarly, make sure it plays to your organization's strengths – in other words, that it is practical and makes good use of your capabilities (as well as those of your suppliers).

2 Ideally, your project should be the solution to a business challenge. For example: how can we launch this new product succesfully? How can we cut costs and maximize opportunities

one minute wonder Before developing a project idea, ask three key questions:

■ **What** does research show our customers or end users need? How will they make use of it?
■ **Why** is this the right project (and is it at the right time) for our organization? How does it fit with our strategy, and with currently available resources?
■ **How** are we (and our suppliers) going to deliver what customers need? What particular skills do we have that make this project the right choice?

What? — Customer/user need
Why? — Business strategy
How? — Team/supplier capability

for collaboration between teams? How can we improve e-communications with our customer base? All these challenges can be the inspiration for a project, such as a marketing plan, a team merger, or a new website.

3 Make sure you have the necessary support in place to get started. Try to view any criticism of your project proposal as constructive – it will help you identify potential risks and pitfalls, and to work out how to reduce the likelihood of these affecting your project.

4 If your project idea doesn't get off the ground, don't be discouraged. The cost of 'closing' your project at this stage is probably very small; this is rarely the case later on, so, by testing your idea before starting, you are likely to have saved a significant amount of money. Treat it is a learning experience and move on. Besides, without creative ideas, there would be no innovation!

Make sure your project idea is absolutely right for your business.

Get creative!

Sometimes turning an initial idea into something more coherent requires a little creative effort. In the process-driven world of projects, this can seem difficult. However, that needn't be the case. There are a number of tools you can use to turn a bright idea into a well-defined outline of your project.

Visual planning

'Mind maps' – diagrams representing ideas and tasks – can be very useful for brainstorming initial project ideas. They can range in complexity from simple spider diagrams to lavishly illustrated versions. They work by engaging both sides of the brain in ordering and prioritizing ideas. They are easy to produce on a sheet of paper or company whiteboard; there are also a number of mind-mapping software packages available (some are even free).

To create a mind map, identify a starting idea or goal, say 'plan a launch party' for your company's new clothing store. Write this in the middle of a sheet of paper. Then identify the 'basic ordering ideas' (perhaps catering, invitations and publicity), around which individual activities can be clustered on the paper. Then identify individual tasks or smaller work areas coming off different lines of activities.

Non-visual planning

Not everyone thinks visually. Some people have an auditory preference (they like to think in words and sounds), while others prefer kinaesthetic communication (they respond best to concrete ideas).

When discussing your project proposal, try listening to the metaphors people use ('it sounds like', 'it feels like' and so on) to determine their preferences. This will help you structure your communications accordingly: for example, people with an auditory preference may find it easy to use a mnemonic to recall the key features of your project. (In Secret 1.3, the phrase **A P**roject **I**s **M**anaged is an example of a mnemonic). Those with a kinaesthetic preference may find it easier to be given a 'walk-through' of your main ideas.

Allowing all ideas during planning

Sometimes an initial project scoping meeting can become adversarial, with several points of view being made. Often it is the most skilfully (or forcefully!) argued approach that is adopted, which may or may not be the best one. You can resist this by using your role as Chair to ensure everyone has their say, and by using a structured questioning approach.

For example, you could invite participants to analyse a proposal from three perspectives:

■ **Dreamer.** What are the possibilities here? What new things can we create?
■ **Critic.** Is this idea really workable? What about the risks and downsides?
■ **Realist.** What steps need to be taken to turn these ideas into reality?

This is known as the 'Disney model', after Walt Disney, who often used this approach. It will give you a measured view of the proposal, and help prevent a planning meeting from descending into adversarial arguments.

Use mind maps and other tools to stimulate creativity.

2.3

SOC it to them!

Once you've sketched an outline of your project, the next step is to document the key points of your project. You will need this in order to get the necessary approval to proceed.

This needn't be a detailed plan of how you're going to achieve everything connected with the project, but should be designed to give your stakeholders (especially those concerned with approving the necessary budget and resources) an idea of what's in store. This document is known as a project brief, scope document or strategic outline case (SOC). Even if you have already been given approval to go ahead (sometimes called a project mandate), there are several reasons why putting together a SOC is important. These include:

1 **Information.** Ahead of a more detailed plan, it gives you a chance to inform your colleagues of what's coming up (though this is no reason not to consider more informal means of communication, such as a staff newsletter).

2 **Approval.** If you haven't yet received a mandate to carry out your project, presenting a 'business case' for your project is a necessary first step. This gives those responsible for approving the necessary expenditure the information they need in one compact document. Your SOC can be circulated in advance of a meeting, where you will have the chance to present your ideas and answer any questions.

3 **Reassurance.** By outlining what your project will and won't deliver, and the resources required, a SOC may help allay fears or concerns that others have about your project. Of course, there is a chance that it may confirm them, so there is no guarantee it will avoid the need to answer awkward questions! But as a more reliable source of information than the 'rumour mill', it will at least ensure that these questions are relevant.

Your SOC doesn't need to be a long essay, but should set out the main points. Include a paragraph or so on each of the following:

■ An outline of the scope (scale) of the project.
■ The benefits it will bring to the business.
■ The benefits to your customers or end users (more on this soon).
■ Any other options considered for delivering these benefits.
■ The budget and other physical resources (office space, computer equipment and so on) required.
■ The main risks your project will face, and how these will be managed.
■ How many people will be on the project team.
■ The approximate timetable.

Remember that those reading the document will probably only have a short time in which to do so – they can always ask for more information if required.

Presenting a business case for your project is often a necessary first step.

Sell the benefits

The feasibility of any project depends largely on being able to say what benefits it will deliver, for both customers and the organization. This is what sales people like to call "selling the sizzle, not the sausages".

The success of a project to deliver, for example, a new organizational database, depends on how well that database will let users access customer information and conduct marketing campaigns, not on how many megabytes of information it contains or parallel searches it can conduct. To understand the benefits your project intends to provide:

■ **Discover stakeholder motivations.** Knowing the priorities of your main stakeholders will give you vital background information to the project. What are the key issues for your customers? What are your organization's strategic objectives? Talk to customers and colleagues, and consult market research and strategic planning documents to find answers to these questions.

■ **Understand the rationale for the project.** This involves asking 'why' as well as 'what', of both customers and the organization. How exactly, for example, will an office move help the organization? (By saving costs, and making communications easier, for example.)

■ **Dig deeper.** Be persistent in asking how each benefit of the project will really make a difference, using a questioning method such as 'five whys' (see Secret 6.6). For example: "In what areas do you hope to save costs, and by how much?"

■ **Be aware of the risks of not carrying out a project.** Sometimes the main reason for undertaking a project is to avoid a business threat rather than take advantage of an opportunity. Launching a new product quickly, for example, may be necessary to avoid a competitor gaining market share by being 'first to market'.

Once you fully understand the benefits your projects will deliver, include these in your SOC as part of ensuring you have the necessary support to move forward with your project.

The Aspire phase of a project

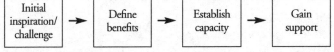

The feasibility of any project depends on what benefits it will deliver.

2.5

Build support

Stakeholder resistance can be based on a lack of understanding of what benefits the project will bring, how it will be accomplished, or how they will be affected by it. As a project manager, you can use certain techniques to understand your stakeholders' concerns, and offer acceptable solutions.

■ **Force field analysis.** This is a tool used to analyse project business cases. It divides the factors affecting a project into opposing 'forces' that either encourage or inhibit change. The weight of each force can then be estimated to determine which is stronger overall. The diagram shows a typical example from a community project, where the analysis clearly (if not overwhelmingly) suggests proceeding with the project.

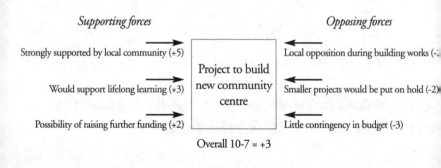

Supporting forces   *Opposing forces*

Strongly supported by local community (+5)   Local opposition during building works (-2)

Would support lifelong learning (+3) | Project to build new community centre | Smaller projects would be put on hold (-2)

Possibility of raising further funding (+2)   Little contingency in budget (-3)

Overall 10-7 = +3

"There are times when the role of the project leader is simply to sell the project' **Sherry Buschmann, NASA**

In *7 Habits of Highly Effective People* (see further reading), Stephen Covey describes two essential features of effective negotiation:

■ **Seek first to understand, then to be understood.** Ideally, you should begin any conversation by listening. Try to understand the concerns that the person objecting to your project has, and what the root causes are. If they are concerned about costs, is this because they do not understand your financial planning sufficiently, or because they are concerened about other budgets for which they are responsible, which may limit the funds available for your project?

■ **Think win/win.** The best solution to any problem is unlikely to be 'win/lose'. Though they may produce short-term results that are in your favour, win/lose discussions often damage precious working relationships, and can become the normal way of 'doing business' – in which case (you)lose/(they)win is always a possibility! Look for a 'third way' that will address stakeholder concerns while keeping the project moving forward.

Know how to build support, even when valid objections are raised, and achieve a win/win solution.

Plan for success

Now you've got the go-ahead, it's time to start planning the project in detail. Your next step should be to compile a project plan. This is also known as a Project Initiation Document, or PID. The project plan builds on the project brief or strategic outline case (SOC), outlined in the previous chapter, to provide a complete picture of how the project will be managed.

3.1

Define your objectives

The first part of your project plan should be a statement of the project's objectives and how these will be realized. It should contain this information:

■ **A 'position statement'.** Explain the background to the project.
■ **The project deliverables.** What tangible outputs your project will produce – a new website, for example, or a launch party for a new club. Essentially this means, "Where do we want to go?"
■ **The key success factors.** The success factors will demonstrate that the project's aims have been achieved. They might include a specification for the new website or a list of the key attendees of your launch party. This means, "How will we know when we've got there?"
■ **Yardsticks.** The various quality indicators that you will use to measure performance.

---

case study Captain Blashford-Smythe was planning a project to reach the North Pole by sled. He listed his key project deliverable (outcome) as "Arrive at the North Pole." His success factors included: "Whole team reaches Pole within sixty days. Enough

---

■ **For a larger project, the key priorities.** This gives a sense of what's really important, and what represents merely the 'icing on the cake'.

■ **What assumptions you are making.** There might be constraints on your project, for example, or the resources available to you (in the latter case, it's always better to have these in writing!).

■ **What has been learned from previous projects.** Focus on what will be useful in delivering this one.

■ **How quality will be assured.** In project parlance, quality generally means being fit for purpose.

Ensure your objectives are SMART:

Specific – quantifiable
Measurable – that quality indicators are in place
Achievable – within the ability of the project team,
        and with the available resources
Relevant – to the current project
Timetabled (see Secret 3.4)

The project's objectives should state clearly what will be achieved.

provisions for return journey. No loss of personnel to polar bears. Only minimal frostbite suffered." The associated quality indicators were: "Compass shows 90° N, 0° W. Quartermaster's statement of provisions. Head count. Team doctor's report."

3.2

Divide the project into work packages

Your first aim is to divide the project up into the main work areas, and then list what needs to be done in each area to create a hierarchical structure of the tasks that need to be carried out in order to deliver your project. This is called a work breakdown structure (WBS for short).

Creating a work breakdown structure consists of three steps.

1 Divide your project up into the principal work packages or work areas. For a software project, for example, these might be: specification, design, implementation, testing, launch.

2 List all the tasks you can think of that will be associated with each work package.

3 Number each task, so that you can identify both main and subsidiary tasks (sub-tasks).

Sample WBS for a new marketing website

1. Project go-ahead
2. Marketing
   2.1 Market research
   2.2 Develop e-commerce model
   2.3 Implement marketing campaign
3. Editorial
   3.1 Specify functionality required
   3.2 Adapt existing content
4. Design
   4.1 Design and test user interface
   4.2 Convert illustrations
5. Technical
   5.1 Arrange contract with host
   5.2 Build database
   5.3 Test database
   5.4 Go-live
   5.5 Write updating manual

6. Human resources
   6.1 Identify HR requirements
   6.2 Recruit temporary staff
   6.3 Build project teams
   6.4 Project teams in place
   6.5 Recruit permanent staff
   6.6 Induct permanent staff
   6.7 Progress monitoring/ training needs analysis
7. Project management
   7.1 Set evaluation criteria/ reporting procedures
   7.2 Monitor and report
   7.3 Handover and inital staff training
   7.4 Final project evaluation and report
8. Project close

Make your WBS as accurate as possible, but don't worry if it isn't complete at this stage. Remember, the best plan is a flexible one! Once you've created a basic WBS, add in some key details that will help you in the next phase, scheduling your project.

■ Identify the likely duration of each task and the resources needed. For example, will it take two software engineers three weeks to build a new database (or three engineers two weeks)?

■ Which of these you choose depends on the constraints that affect your project. How many people are available to work on your project team? Are there certain tasks that cannot begin before a certain date, or must finish by another, because of staff holidays, weather conditions, or other factors outside your control?

Identify work areas and create a work breakdown structure (WBS).

3.3

First things first (and last things last)

Now you know what needs to be done, the next step is to establish the required running order. An easy way to establish this is via a backward pass through the project tasks, then make a diagram to show how all the tasks in the project relate to one another.

■ **Perform a backward pass.** Ask yourself: "What needs to be done immediately before I can do this?" Start at the end and keep going until you reach the beginning. For example, for a project to launch a new company website, the final task is likely to be 'switch servers and go live'. Before this, you need to 'complete testing', and so on. This process is called identifying *dependent* or *precedent* tasks.

■ **Identify the dependency level.** Some tasks can be undertaken independently while others may depend on two or more precedent tasks being completed. Not every precedent task will need to be fully completed before you can start the next one. For example, on a building project, it's likely that interior decoration can start before the electrical work is complete. This type of dependency is called start-to-start (SS), as opposed to the usual finish-to-start (FS) type. Some dependent tasks of this type require a delay before they can start, which is called lag time.

■ **Draw a network diagram.** You can draw a network diagram on a sheet of paper, but you may find it easier to use one of the software packages described in Chapter 1, as these will make it easier to make modifications should the need arise. By plotting the longest path through the network without retracing your steps, a network diagram can be used to determine how long it is expected for the project to be completed. These tasks occupy what is known as the critical path: their durations cannot be increased without affecting the overall schedule. Tasks that do not occupy the critical path have what is known as slack or float time: the amount of slack time determines how late they can run before they appear on the critical path and affect the project duration.

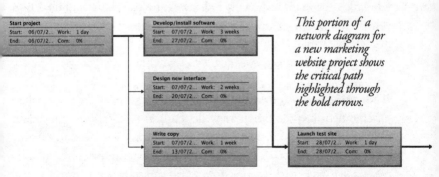

This portion of a network diagram for a new marketing website project shows the critical path highlighted through the bold arrows.

Identify the critical path your project needs to take.

3.4

Build a project timetable

Once you've established the task order and project duration, you can create a realistic timetable that enables everyone to understand where they need to be, and when.

A Gantt chart is often used as a way of showing the project timetable. Named after the American engineer Henry Gantt, this shares many of the same features as a network diagram, but the emphasis is on scheduling as much as showing task relationships. Though all the major project management software programs can display Gantt charts, for

one minute wonder Once your schedule is confirmed, save a copy. This is then known as the baseline schedule. This will enable you to compare progress against a target as the project progresses. Of course, if major changes occur before the project begins, you can create a new baseline.

Example Gantt chart for a CD project

Date: w/c	6-Sep-10	13-Sep-10	20-Sep-10	27-Sep-10	4-Oct-10
ACTIVITY					
Recording	•	•			
Cover design		•	•		
Mixing				•	
Production					•

smaller projects they can be easily created using Excel or similar spreadsheet software. There are various ways of filling them in. The simple Gantt chart above uses dots to indicate when different activities are needed during a schedule to create a commercial CD.

■ **Import task information.** Import the task information (duration, dependencies and so on) from your work breakdown structure and network diagram into your timetable.

■ **Allow for time constraints.** Identify any further constraints that may affect the timing of the project. For example, during an office move project, this might include the availability of new premises. Alternatively, during a construction project, a key team (say electricians) might not be available after a certain date. Use this information to add earliest start or latest finish dates where appropriate.

Draw up a project timetable for everyone working on the project to see how they fit into the schedule.

3.5

Add contingency and use it wisely

When setting task durations, add some contingency – extra time – where possible, especially to those tasks that are vulnerable to delay. This will help avoid overrun, also known as schedule slippage.

Contingency needs to be managed: be sure how much you are including, and why, otherwise it may look as if you are simply allowing extra time to do the work. Ways of managing contingency include:

■ **Planning for interruptions.** A task that should take five continuous days (photographing fashionwear as part of a retail catalogue project, for example) might suffer interruptions due to bad weather, causing it to take eight days; in this case it is better to set eight days rather than five as the task duration.

"If anything can go wrong, it will"

'Murphy's Law' adage

one minute wonder According to Harvey Levine, founder of the Project Knowledge Group, there are three things you can be sure of. First: if there is no schedule contingency, the project end date will be missed. Second: if the contingency is not managed, the schedule will slip and you will finish even later. Third: Murphy [i.e. the founder of 'Murphy's Law' – see opposite] is working on your project!

■ **Anticipating any delays between tasks.** Where these are likely to occur, you can deal with this by setting a finish-to-start time lag (see Secret 3.3).

■ **Sharing contingency between tasks.** Create a task called 'contingency' that covers a range of (real) tasks. This can be used as required to reduce the likelihood of 'Parkinson's Law' occurring, where work expands to fill the available time!

Where necessary, set a fairly challenging latest finish date for a given task, to focus your team on early completion.

Contingency is also helpful when budgeting – see Chapter 4.

Once the project is in progress, it is important to know how much contingency has been used, and why. For more on using contingency as part of progress monitoring, see Chapter 6.

Once the project is in progress, it is important to know how much contingency has been used, and why.

3.6

Match people to tasks

Having identified the order of activities and set a timetable, the next step is to allocate people to tasks. This will enable you to get everyone working on the right activities at the right time, and to identify where you may need to bring in extra resources or adjust the schedule.

■ **Some tasks are of fixed duration.** This doesn't necessarily mean that there is no doubt over how long they will take, merely that you cannot control them. For example, obtaining planning permission for a new building generally takes a fixed amount of time regardless of how many people you have working on it.

■ **Other tasks are effort-driven.** This means how long they take depends on how many people are involved, and for how long. For example, if it takes ten software engineers three weeks to create a new hospital record system, then it would take five software engineers (half as many) six weeks (twice as long).

Knowing how many 'man-hours' are required for each task allows you to decide whether to recruit an in-house team or if all or part of your team should be composed of freelancers. Use this information as part of the overall project costing.

■ **Creating a resource histogram.** Using the scheduling information in your Gantt chart, you can work how many people need to be available at a particular time to work on your project. Show this in a bar chart called a resource histogram. A resource histogram can be a useful way of highlighting when your resource team is overcommitted (scheduled to be in two places at once).

Example resource histogram for a website project

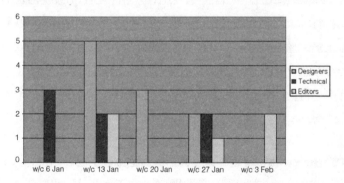

If a team member is overcommitted you can do one of two things. Either bring in extra resources, to get the task done on time (which is likely to affect the project budget), or amend the project schedule, to allow your team member to complete one task before he starts another (which may affect the schedule). The process of amending the schedule to take account of resource limitations is known as resource levelling or resource smoothing.

Allocating people to tasks helps you identify any need for extra resources.

3.7

Organize and control your project

An essential part of planning any project is identifying how the project will be organized and decisions made. How will you communicate with your project team and monitor progress? Just as importantly, how will you involve the project sponsor and stakeholders?

Areas that need to be covered include:

■ **Team meetings and project reporting.** How often will you meet with the project team, what reports will you ask for, and how should problems or issues be raised?

■ **Quality control.** How is 'quality' defined: what evidence is needed for you to see if a task has been done properly?

■ **Managing stage boundaries.** Once a milestone has been reached, what is the process for moving on to the next stage?

■ **Change control.** If amendments to the schedule need to be made, or extra people brought in, how will this be managed?

■ **Tolerance.** Most projects will allow for a certain level of change to be authorized directly by the project manager – this margin is known as tolerance. Setting the right level of tolerance involves balancing the relative weight of risk and agility factors.

■ **Project organization.** For example, PRINCE2™ specifies the creation of a project board to oversee the project. (For more on project perspectives, see Secret 1.5)

■ **Management by exception.** The project manager should communicate regularly with the project board or sponsor, who will normally only be asked to 'manage by exception' – that is, only asked to comment or act on problems or variances from the original plan.

Example organization diagram for a website project

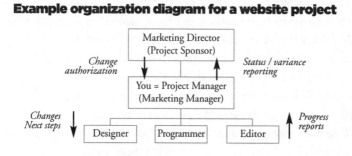

Decide how you will communicate with your team and monitor progress.

3.8

Manage risks wisely

Managing risk is one of the most important parts of a project manager's job. Knowing how and when things might go wrong, and taking steps to minimize the negative effects on your project, are essential. Good risk management can make the difference between a viable and a non-viable project.

■ **Risk assessment.** Every project plan should incorporate a risk assessment. This documents the likelihood of each potential adverse incident occurring, the severity of the impact if any of these were to occur and the measure needed to reduce likelihood and limit damage.

■ **External and internal risks.** External risks come from outside the project team, and include changes in markets, environmental conditions and legislation. Internal risks stem from the project team: training gaps and skill shortages, culture and personality clashes, and failures in supplier management, for example.

■ **Establishing your exposure to risk.** By quantifying the overall exposure you face to each risk, your risk assessment can be used to target effort where it is most needed (see Table opposite).

■ **Unavoidable risks.** Some risks are unavoidable – for example, 'bugs' during software development. These are often (somewhat obliquely) described as 'issues'. Rather than prevent issues occurring (which is

> **"The rule of military operations is not to count on opponents not coming, but to rely on having ways of dealing with them"** Sun Tzu, 'The Art of War', 6th century BC

probably impossible), the best strategy is to have a plan for dealing with them when they arise.

■ **'Hard' benefits.** The 'hard' benefits of risk management are tangible improvements in areas such as the reliability of budgets and schedules, discouraging financially unsound projects, allocating responsibility for risk to the most appropriate person or organization and providing a better platform for future business.

■ **'Soft' benefits.** 'Soft' benefits include a common understanding of the the project environment, highlighting the most important issues for the project and organization, demonstrating responsibility and improved customer relations.

Sample risk assessment diagram for a marketing DVD project

Risk	Likelihood	Impact	Exposure	Indicators	Actions
Wrong video encoding system used	High	High	Very high	Plays only on some test machines	Specify full list of operating systems
Poor navigation / interface	Medium	High	High	Frequent technical support calls	Thorough testing
Late editorial changes	Medium	Medium	Medium	Delays / cost overruns	Agree schedule / sign-off procedures
Poor distribution	Low	Medium	Low	High return rate	Clean contact database

Good risk management can make the difference between a viable and a non-viable project.

3.9

'Design in' quality

The process of ensuring that all the elements of the project plan contribute to its ultimate success involves planning for quality. This means setting a quality benchmark for individual tasks or 'work packages' (groups of tasks), so that the end result of each task conforms to a minimum specification. Here are five key steps to incorporating quality.

1 **Be aware of external quality standards.** These might include international quality standards, such as ISO 9000; national and local health and safety regulations; international environmental standards, such as ISO 1400; national employment legislation.

2 **Define quality specifications for each product.** During the project there will be a number of 'products' to be produced, whether it is a new database built as part of a new e-commerce project, or a new shop-front design as part of a store refurbishment programme. Talk to experts within the field about what constitutes a high-quality product, and include this in your quality specification.

"Quality is remembered long after the price is forgotten"

Gucci family slogan

3 **Determine the 'cost of quality'.** Both quality itself, and the quality assurance process, carry costs. To build the maximum possible quality product every time, and to go through the most rigorous possible checking process, might increase costs unecessarily. The process of determining what 'quality' means for your project involves finding out what the customer wants, what the supplier is able to provide, and what the project budget can afford.

4 **Put in place procedures for monitoring quality.** Having a sophisticated quality assurance plan is no use without good-quality data to feed into it. Make sure both those whose work will be measured, and those who will be doing the measuring, know how the process is to work.

5 **Plan to report quality.** It's important to know how quality information will be communicated, whether in exception reporting, or as part of a balanced scorecard (see Secret 6.5). This will help to ensure that your efforts at assuring quality result in any necessary changes to the plan being made as the project progresses.

Planning for quality means setting a quality benchmark for individual tasks or work packages.

Manage
your money

Project budgeting is often given comparatively little attention. Areas like scheduling and team leadership can be seen as more glamorous ways for a project manager to spend his or her time. Though this is understandable, it is a little odd. Firstly, because delivering on budget is one of the key success factors for any project; secondly, because finance and most other areas of project and resource management are inextricably linked.

4.1

Understand the role of finance

Maintaining financial awareness is essential at all stages of your project. It will help you see the bigger picture and to zoom in on details where necessary. The two essential elements of good financial management of any project are accurate cost estimation during planning and rigorous cost control during implementation. These stages can be broken down as explained here.

■ **Project brief.** Even if it contains no actual cost information, a project brief will help you estimate an overall cost range by outlining the scope (scale) of the project.

■ **Work breakdown structure.** Your WBS should contain detailed information about the time and people needed to carry out each project. This will enable you to build a provisional estimate of the project's costs.

■ **Contract negotiation.** This part of the process provides an opportunity to minimize costs by careful evaluation of supplier tender documents (bids for work) and the selection of appropriate types of supplier contract.

"Money is rarely a problem; it's the absence of money that is a problem. Negative money is something to worry about"

Geoff Reiss, project management writer and trainer

■ **Project budget.** Once people are allocated to tasks and supplier contracts confirmed, you are in a position to confirm the project costs. These estimates can then be locked or *baselined* as a basis for future comparison. (See Secret 4.7 for more on cost baselining).

■ **Cost control.** Once the project is underway, the emphasis changes to one of monitoring and reporting costs, ensuring cost changes receive the necessary authorization, and amending the project budget where necessary.

■ **Evaluating return on investment (ROI).** Once the project is complete, the project manager's role is to compare costs with outcomes, to ensure that the project has delivered value for money.

Summary of the role of finance in project management

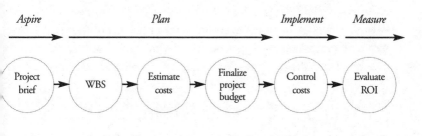

Always compare costs with outcomes.

Estimate project costs

Managing project finances is another key element of the project manager's role. Building a clear and accurate picture of likely costs is essential.

1 Take the time to understand each task involved. This will give you a more complete insight into what is required financially.

2 Understand your company's internal charging policy. If staff from another team are being seconded to work on your project, will the project be charged for their time?

3 For work that needs to be undertaken outside of your company, prepare a competitive tender that will enable multiple suppliers to bid. (There is more on this in the next Secrets.)

"Trust is not just an attitude that is nice to have. It is a must, since a lack of trust costs money"

Judy Stokley, Project Manager, US Air Force

4 Talk to colleagues who have undertaken similar projects, to find out how much they have paid.

5 Understand your suppliers' motivations for wanting to bid on your contract – this will help you negotiate the best deal. It's true your suppliers will need to make a profit. However, they will also have other motivations, such as the desire to build a reputation for quality and reliability in the market in which you operate.

6 Be creative. If a task is proving too expensive, can it be done differently, or be omitted altogether?

7 Don't bow to pressure to present unrealistically low cost estimates. This may get you through a tricky conversation, but is likely to store up trouble for later. Remember the project triangle – reducing costs is likely to result in lower quality.

8 Remember that time and costs are generally linked – if your project overruns by a week, this will probably mean a week's extra pay for the project team.

9 Manage cashflow as well as costs – many projects that fail do so because they run out of money in the short term.

10 Allocate some budget contingency to deal with unforeseeen overspends. Create a shared contingency budget for each work package, and a tight budget for tasks prone to overspending.

It is important to describe in your project plan how costs will be monitored and controlled as the project progresses.

Work out all possible costs in advance.

4.3

Choose to insource or outsource

Cost plays a major role in deciding whether to use personnel from within your organization or to recruit freelance personnel. These are the main points to consider when selecting whether to 'insource' or 'outsource' your project team.

■ **Skills.** Is there sufficient expertise in-house, or do you need to recruit outside specialists?

■ **Internal vs external costs.** Can existing staff be used at no cost to the project, or will internal re-charging apply? If so, how will these costs compare with employing contractors (freelancers)? Will your team be office-based or virtual, and will this affect your decision?

case study In Alex Laufer and Edward Hoffman's 'Project Management Success Stories – Lessons of Project Leaders' (see further reading), George Hurt of the US Air Force describes how he could not get his project off the ground. In trying to specify a new back-up system for the Space Shuttle, those commissioning the new system were demanding such a long list of

■ **Start-up.** Assuming they have the necessary skills, is it likely that existing staff could get 'up and running' more easily, due to their knowledge of organizational procedures and culture, or would freelance team members' familiarity with project working mean they adapt more quickly?

■ **Commitment.** Who would be more committed to the project: existing staff who understand the values of the organization and might want the chance to learn valuable extra skills, or freelance contractors, who want to enhance their professional reputation?

■ **Learning.** Will any new skills learnt or new processes developed during the project be lost when the project team is disbanded, if the team consisted chiefly of freelance contractors? Or is the plan for evaluating the project sufficiently robust to prevent this happening?

■ **Intellectual property.** Do your freelance contracts make clear that the copyright of any inventions or new business processes developed during the project belongs to the organization rather than an individual?

■ **Politics.** If using an internally recruited project team is the best approach, staff will need to be seconded from their existing teams to work on your project. Do you know how you will negotiate this? Are there any foreseeable barriers to internal recruitment, and how would these be overcome?

Find the right balance between in-house and freelance staff.

safety standards, and setting such exhaustive testing requirements, that he felt delivery was impossible. His answer? Appoint half the project team from the customer side! That way they could be in no doubt that their concerns were being addressed, and they were able to agree a more practical approach to developing the new system.

4.4

Choose the right supplier

Not all tasks can be undertaken in-house. Let's say you are producing a marketing brochure: the writing and editing can be done in-house, along with the design if you have the capability. The printing, however, will need to be undertaken externally by a specialist printer.

Choosing the right supplier can save costs and may also give you a better quality product, and/or faster service. Supplier selection and management is important in managing both costs and quality. This process is known as procurement. There are several things you can do to ensure an effective procurement strategy:

1 Identify the best cost basis for the work package at hand. For example, providing pens and paper with your company logo, as part of a project to produce a conference pack, will carry a fixed cost. (The activity of purchasing them may be effort-driven, but is likely to be a very small task not worth recording on the project plan.) See the next Secret for more on supplier contracts and costs.

"Trust in, microrequire-ments out"

George Hurt, US Air Force, on dealing with suppliers

2 Draw up a shortlist of suppliers and send each of these a speci-fication of the task or work package that needs to be undertaken, with a closing date for responses.

3 Once you have received supplier bids (tenders), evaluate these against a range of quality criteria.

Product/service quality criteria can include price, specification and delivery time. Supplier quality criteria can include financial stabil-ity, reliability, responsiveness, experience of working on similar projects, and commitment to your market area.

You can check most of these criteria from the tender documents received. To explore issues like reliability and responsiveness, ask for references, and follow these up with a phone call or site visit. If the work being outsourced is a major component of the project, consider inter-viewing a shortlist of bidders before making your final decision.

Effective procurement is an important part of managing costs and quality.

4.5

Negotiate the right type of contract

To work effectively with your suppliers, and to ensure they deliver value for money, you need to negotiate the most appropriate type of contract for your project. There are two factors to consider: contract scope (what it covers) and contract cost basis.

The three main types of contract scope are:

■ **Turnkey.** With this type of contract, the product or service is built, tested and delivered into the client's care. The contract ends at this point and the product becomes the client's responsibility. Examples of turnkey projects range from contract publishing to building a mansion.

■ **Build–Operate–Train–Handover (BOTH).** Here the contract runs on beyond design and delivery of the finished product, into a handover period. An example of a project suitable for BOTH would be a new company database.

■ **Build–Operate–Own–Maintain (BOOM).** In this case the emphasis shifts towards a longer-term involvement on the part of the supplier. Examples of BOOM contracts range from photocopiers to complex medical equipment.

"A verbal contract isn't worth the paper it's written on"

Samuel Goldwyn, film producer

The different contract cost types are:

■ **Fixed cost.** In this type of contract, the specification and price are fixed in advance. No matter what happens at the supplier's end – such as unforeseen extensions to the task duration or complexity that are not a result of changes to the project scope, such as an increase in the cost of raw materials or transport, or higher labour rates – the cost to the project remains the same. This offers the reassurance of a fixed rate (though beware of hidden 'contingency').

■ **Rate-based.** Here, the supplier charges an agreed hourly or daily rate and the final bill is calculated once the task is complete. This method makes it harder to predict the overall cost, but can be used when changes in scope are widely expected.

■ **Cost-plus.** In this case the supplier charges a rate based on his or her own costs, with an additional premium to allow them a profit margin. This is similar to rate-based charging, though it is more transparent.

■ **Maximum price.** With a maximum price contract, the supplier offers rate-based or cost-plus pricing, but guarantees a maximum price ceiling. This makes it easier to set a firm project budget. Assuming the maximum cost is higher than your estimate of the most likely figure, you can automatically include some contingency.

In choosing both contract scope and cost type, your supplier's views may differ from your own, so be prepared to negotiate!

To work well with your suppliers, you need an effective contract.

Make a return on your investment

Some projects will be expected to make a profit. In these cases, estimating and then generating financial returns may be part of the project manager's job. These are some of the key measures to include.

If your project aims to make a profit, you will be able to forecast a financial return on investment (ROI). You can calculate ROI as a percentage using the following formula:

$$ROI = (profit \div investment) \times 100$$

If you are generating a product or service that can be resold, rather than a single product for which you will receive a payment, you can estimate the payback period for the money invested in the project. This is the point at which the income generated by the project matches the project costs.

case study John is office manager at a distribution company. He was asked to manage a project to relocate his company's offices into a single, purpose-built site. A key aim of the project was to save on rental

For example, you are the manager of a project that has a $10,000 budget to produce a yoga DVD for a chain of gymnasiums. The DVD will be sold for $20, and sales are forecast of 50 units per month – equivalent to 600 units in the first year (total $12,000).

■ To generate sufficient sales to match the project costs, you need to sell 500 DVDs ($10,000 ÷ $20 = 500), which works out to a payback period of 10 months (500 DVDs ÷ 50 per month = 10 months).

When calculating payback period (and even ROI, on a long-term project), your accounts manager may ask you to discount the income by a percentage. This is to cover interest that could have been had from simply investing the project costs.

■ If the interest rate is 5%, this would mean that your net income (the amount by which the sales income exceeds the amount that would have been earned by simply investing the money) can be calculated as (500 x $20 x 0.95) = $9,500. This makes the payback period about 10 and a half months.

You may feel that the main benefits of your project are not financial and this is perfectly fine. There are many different ways in which a project can deliver benefits to your organization.

Work out the payback period for your project.

costs. He negotiated a new lease that cost $50,000 per year less than the previous total. The overall cost of the office move was $100,000, so the payback period was two years.

4.7

Freeze the project budget

Once your project cost estimates are completed and any supplier contracts drawn up, the next step is to finalize the project budget. This brings together the costs and any income estimates for the project, and sets out how the project costs will be allocated.

Your project budget should answer the following questions:

■ **How much will the project cost overall?** This will be a single total.

■ **How will project costs be allocated across various work areas?** (These are often known as cost centres.) You can display this on a spreadsheet or one of the cost breakdown sheets provided with any project management software package.

■ **How do costs need to be phased during the life of the project?** This will depend on the nature of the relationship with your suppliers, contractors and team members. Suppliers of goods and services will require payment within a set period from delivery (often 30 days); contractors undertaking long-term work on the project may require stage payments as individual elements of the work are completed; freelance project team members will require monthly or weekly payment.

If you need to show when payments need to be made (and therefore how much of the project budget is left), you can do this by means of a cashflow forecast.

Many projects are concerned with generating an end product rather than income, which tends to be part of a wider programme or business plan. However, it is not always the case that projects only have costs associated with them, so show any income forecasts associated with the project together with the headline costs for each work area. Accountants call this a profit and loss account.

Example final project budget for a marketing DVD

Costs ($)	Projected	Income ($)	Projected
Design	750	Sponsorship	5,000
Rights/royalties	250		
Coding	1,000	Less DVD costs	3,650
Testing	400		
Production (500)	1,000	Net profit	1,350
Distribution	250		
Total	3,650		

Bring together the cost and any income estimates for the project.

4.8

Control costs

Once the project is underway, your focus should shift from cost estimation to cost control. Successfully controlling project costs involves three distinct activities: keeping as far as possible within budget, feeding information about actual costs back into the project budget, and identifying the causes of any variations.

The key to staying within the budgeted cost for any task is to ensure an accurate and timely flow of cost information from the project team. This will enable you to react swiftly to any signs of financial trouble. It also acts as a reminder to the project team of the importance you attach to working within budget.

case study Alex was working on a project to deliver a new website for her organization, a medium-sized charity. The site design came in on budget, as did most of the programming. It was when she moved onto linking the website with the charity's donor database that the problems began. There were delays, and bills started appearing for extra costs from both the web designers and the database suppliers. She spoke to

■ If an activity runs over budget, update the project budget to show the actual cost and to highlight the cost variance. This will keep everyone up-to-date and informed.

■ With your project team, identify the reason for the cost variance. This will help you establish whether this was a one-off occurrence, or if the cost overrun is the result of an underlying issue that needs addressing (such as a skills gap within the project team, or a lack of communication) or if it is likely to reoccur. You can then agree an action plan to reduce the likelihood of future cost overruns.

■ If the cost overrun emanates from a supplier, include them in an open discussion about the reasons why, and ways to limit reoccurrence.

■ If the cost variance is within the tolerance limits set out in your project plan, you can move on, using the wisdom you have gained to reduce the likelihood of future cost overruns. If the variance falls outside the agreed tolerance limits, you will need to obtain change authorization from the project board or project commissioner.

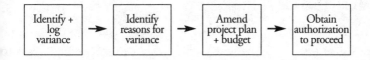

| Identify + log variance | → | Identify reasons for variance | → | Amend project plan + budget | → | Obtain authorization to proceed |

Keep monitoring your budget when the project gets underway.

each individually: "It's not our fault, it's more complicated than we thought", came the reply in each case. "We want X but they supply Y" said the web agency. "We do Y. X is their job" replied the database people. To move things forward, Alex invited both suppliers to a meeting. They both agreed that they had not looked at the detail previously and would collaborate on a joint specification from that point onwards.

Lead and inspire your team

It's people, rather than processes, that really get results in projects. While good procedures and adequate resources are important, they can't produce results on their own. Many a poorly resourced project has been delivered successfully by teams with the inspiration, dedication and leadership to succeed.

5.1

Design in success to your project team

The first step in building a high-performing project team is to recruit the right people. Then you can begin building them into a group of people who will deliver your project successfully.

According to researchers at Harvard Business School (and they should know) a team is a 'small number of people with complementary skills who are committed to a common purpose, performance goals and a common approach, for which they hold themselves mutually accountable'. Try to build these features into your team from the outset. To do this, follow these three steps:

case study Polar explorer Ernest Shackleton, one of the great leaders of the 20th century, imparted a strong vision to the crew of the HMS Endeavour when they were marooned on the ice in an Antarctic winter. The 'project' was getting them home safely without loss of life. Throughout their epic voyage, first across ice and then rough, cold seas, he continually reminded them of their aim by providing examples of

1 **Build a shared team vision.** The Ancient Chinese military strategist Sun Tzu remarked on the need for each team's vision to be aligned with those of the wider organization (in his case an army). A high-performing team has a clear understanding of what constitutes its work and why this is important. Give your team an answer to the question: "Where are we headed, and why?"

2 **Motivate your team to achieve.** Research shows that people are motivated by two different types of reward: intrinsic (internal) rewards include doing a job well, acquiring new skills, and 'winning'; extrinsic (external) rewards include pay, acclaim and respect. Understand what motivates your team and you will be able to design a suitable package of incentives.

3 **Cultivate 'esprit'.** 'Esprit' is the soul of a team. An indicator of esprit is when people begin using "we" more than "I". Use team-building activities – anything from a work-based game to sports or social activities – to create this sense of shared identity.

Choose people who are likely to work together well, and build a sense of shared identity.

selflessness, including discarding his gold watch and other personal possessions to save weight. Despite his single-minded determination, he also appreciated the vital importance of morale in maintaining performance: possessions saved included a crew member's banjo. Despite suffering the most severe hardships for several months, the entire party managed to return safely to civilization.

5.2

Understand team dynamics

Managing the growth and development of your team effectively is essential if you are to avoid confusion and 'drift'. Like projects, teams have growth cycles. You need to be able to identify and react to these.

■ **Put together a 'team jigsaw'.** This means ensuring that team members have the necessary skills and will work together successfully.

■ **Bridge the gaps.** Psychologists have developed a number of tools that can be used to measure 'team fit' (as opposed to individual aptitude). Ask your personnel department if there is a particular team profiling model in use within your organization.

case study Another example from 'Project Management Success Stories' tells how Don and Dave, two NASA engineers, were working late at night to test components that were to be used in space – at temperatures close to absolute zero. Suddenly their laboratory was hit by a power cut. This was potentially serious: soon their refrigeration equipment would cease

■ **Consider the Belbin model.** Perhaps the easiest profiling model is Belbin team role profiling (named after the management academic of the same name). This involves asking each of your team members to complete a questionnaire to establish their natural roles within a team. Belbin and similar team profiling methods are a helpful way of identifying the natural strengths and weaknesses within your team, enabling you to modify roles and working methods accordingly.

■ **Accelerate team growth.** According to research carried out by Bruce Tuckman, the search for roles and goals produces a recognizable pattern of team development. He describes these four stages as:

> **Forming** – an initial 'honeymoon' period, with team roles and purpose as not yet defined.
> **Storming** – jostling for position, with clarity of purpose unlikely, but team roles not fully defined.
> **Norming** – mutual trust and confidence grow; the beginnings of shared leadership emerge.
> **Performing** – a high level of mutual understanding means that the team is now significantly greater than the sum of its parts.

A successful team depends on complementary, rather than conflicting, roles.

to function, ruining weeks of work. After some head-scratching, they came up with an innovative solution. Starting with two 12-volt radio batteries, they created a temporary back-up generator that saw them through until power was restored. Rex, the project's manager, reported that disaster would have occurred were it not for Don and Dave's dedication and resourcefulness.

5.3

Make the most of matrix working

As more organizations adopt a project approach, they are using dedicated project teams drawn from across the organization. This is known as matrix working.

An in-house team uses existing staff capacity, so is generally easier on the project budget. As mentioned, established staff members can generally be expected to understand both your organization's vision and mission, and therefore see the project in a corporate context, which may yield valuable results. Their knowledge of company culture may also streamline interaction with the wider organization.

To make the most of matrix working, be prepared to champion your project to colleagues throughout the organization:

■ **Managers of other teams.** Where staff have been seconded from other teams to work on your project, their managers may feel aggrieved that they have been deprived of valuable staff. Stress to them the benefits of your project to the whole organization (and ask the project commissioner to do so). To avoid this problem, more and more organizations are, as part of adopting a project approach, allowing for matrix working during their annual business planning cycles.

one minute wonder Use the stakeholder mapping process described in Secret 1.4 to highlight who in your organization will be most affected by matrix working on your project. You can then plan a communication strategy. For example, if fellow team managers are worried about their own departments becoming short-staffed, you could stress the long-term benefits of the new skills team members will gain.

■ **Project team members.** Seconding (borrowing) the most suitably qualified staff to work on your project may mean you are employing team members who 'outrank' you. Adapt your management style accordingly, by delegating tasks that team members with more expertise can work on semi-autonomously, and draw on their experience in team meetings. As project manager, though, you will need the courage to remind them of their team responsibility, if necessary.

■ **Colleagues of project team members.** People who are not employed on the project may feel resentful to have been denied opportunities on what they may see as a glamorous diversion from their day job! Explain that the project team has been selected on the basis of the precise skills needed; or emphasize the importance of the work they are doing within their existing team.

■ **Senior management.** You can only do so much to stress the benefits of your project to other senior managers. Ultimately, matrix project management requires genuine senior management support.

Understand the implications of matrix working on other teams.

5.4

Tailor your leadership style

Traditional management approaches often tend to emphasize 'leading from the front': this is sometimes the right thing to do, as a team needs direction and guidance. Sometimes, however, a better approach is 'leading from the middle'. Set goals and assign roles, but do so in a way that resonates with the beliefs, values and motivations of team members.

In *Engaging Leadership* (see further reading) three 'agendas' are described that leaders need to establish with their teams:

■ **Intellectual agenda.** Invite your team to a discussion about your project's aims, based on transparency and a shared understanding of roles and goals.

■ **Behavioural agenda.** As a leader, your behaviour reveals your beliefs and values. Be a role model for your team by listening actively in discussions, offering support and constructive challenge.

■ **Emotional agenda.** A strong sense of purpose is acquired as much by achieving the right frame of mind as by any logical means of persuasion. Challenge your team to create the passion necessary to 'go for it'.

"One's determination will lead to others' success"

Harun Al-Rashid, 9th-century caliph

Manage the person, not the task. Projects are governed by processes, so it is perhaps not surprising that project managers can sometimes default to issuing task directives rather than identifying the necessary level of advice and support to offer. Hersey and Blanchard's model of 'situational leadership' describes how leaders need to adopt a flexible leadership style – one that reflects the level of competence and commitment of a team member when confronted with a particular task. These four leadership styles as known as:

■ **Telling.** A person new to a task will need close guidance.
■ **Coaching.** As their expertise increases, they will increasingly be able to input into how things are done.
■ **Supporting.** Once they are proficient in their role, decision-making becomes a joint task between you and the team member.
■ **Delegating.** A fully competent and confident team member can be given control of their job; your role as team leader is to offer support and advice when required.

Mentoring and coaching are two distinct roles for a team leader. Mentoring involves offering advice based on your own experience. By contrast, coaching consists of talking through issues and helping people to deal with them using their own (often hidden) strengths. The emphasis is on listening and asking relevant questions rather than dispensing advice. Develop your skills in both these areas, and you will increase your value as a leader.

Lead from the middle, not the front.

5.5

Communication is more than just words

Effective communication as a basis for building good working relationships and resolving conflicts is vital in promoting productive team working. The essence of good communication is listening to others – remember that communication is an art, not a science.

Begin by asking questions to determine what the issue is, and you will generally find an appropriate response. For example, if someone asks you for your views on how they are progressing with a task, do they want a detailed critique or are they just looking for reassurance that you are happy with their work?

Have you ever walked into a meeting and decided something was wrong before anything was said? When Charlie promised that the database programming would be finished by tomorrow, did something make you suspect otherwise?

Experts have suggested that communication has three aspects:

1 **Physiological ('body language').** Posture, gestures and breathing contain up to half of the information we receive in a conversation. For example, does this person look relaxed or agitated?

"The problem with communication is the illusion that it has occurred" George Bernard Shaw, Irish playwright

Voice-dependent. Up to a third of communication is voice-dependent. The tone of voice and speed of delivery someone is using are also strong clues to their state of mind. Do they sound happy or sad, uninterested or excited?

Verbal. The 'subject matter' of a conversation is of course important, but may amount to less than a quarter of the information received.

Be aware of the powerful non-verbal aspects of a conversation, both when speaking and listening. Look for 'congruence', when body language, voice and content are in harmony with one another.

■ **Use appropriate metaphors.** As mentioned in Chapter 2, people 'model' the world in different ways. Understanding what communication model – auditory, visual or kinaesthetic (feeling) – someone prefers will provide a clue to what metaphors will appeal to a particular person. Try listening to how they habitually describe a situation: "It looks to me as if…", "This sounds like" or "It feels like", and tailor your communication style effectively. (See Secret 2.2 for more on how to use metaphors in project communication.)

■ **Tell stories.** Anecdotes or examples – either from previous projects or other areas of life – are a powerful way of getting a point across.

Effective communication can make a huge difference in all areas of business.

5.6

Learn to manage difficult conversations

Perhaps you feel a team member is not pulling his or her weight, or two of your team members are not getting on, which is affecting their productivity and morale across the team. There are three steps to managing these potentially difficult conversations.

1 **Use the right language.** Communication difficulties can arise between what training expert Shelle Rose Charvet calls a 'process' person (who wants to get things done, and to know the outcome) and a 'people' person (who wants to know how something feels to another, and its significance to them). Begin by taking the time to understand which category each of the

case study Tim was faced with a tricky situation with Alice, a senior colleague who 'outranked' him, and had been seconded to Tim's project team for her IT knowledge. Alice often expressed strong opinions on non-IT issues, which Tim felt was having a destabilizing effect on the team. Tim asked to meet Alice over a coffee,

people in your team belongs to (and who is a mixture of both). Then use language that will appeal to that type of person to ensure that what you say has relevance to them.

2 **Use logical levels.** British anthropologist Gregory Bateson coined the term 'logical levels' to describe the various levels at which people think. At the lower levels, motivation is relatively superficial: "What should I do, and where?" At the higher levels, questions become deeper: "Do I believe in what I'm doing?" Difficult conversations arise when participants mix logical levels – for example, one person talks about what they believe in, while another speaks in terms of what they should do and how. Use precise language: "I think you need to communicate more effectively with colleagues; try talking to them face-to-face rather than emailing them" (a behavioural issue) is more specific, and less likely to meet with resistance, than: "I don't think you're a good communicator" (challenging someone's identity).

3 **Maintain the relationship if at all possible.** Sometimes communication becomes negative, defensive or focused on blame. If so, you should focus on neutral issues where you can find common ground, so that you can begin to constructively address areas of difference. Only consider removing the team member if their dishonesty or misconduct forces you to.

Know how to deal with conflicts.

and they began by discussing their families and holidays. Tim then explained that he valued Alice's role as an IT expert but was concerned about her antagonistic views on other issues. Alice agreed in future to discuss any major concerns with Tim in private rather than with other team members.

5.7

Manage yourself, then the project

As leader of your project, you are a role model for the team and the most visible symbol of how the project is being run. How you behave at criticial moments in the project, from launch to closure, will contribute to how your team and wider stakeholders view the project, and possibly how they behave themselves.

These are are four ways in which you can become an effective role model for your project team:

1 **Be proactive.** In *7 Habits of Highly Effective People* (see further reading), Stephen Covey advocates 'response-ability' – being able to choose a response to a difficult situation. If you have a clear sense of purpose about your project and a strong vision of what you want to achieve, use this to help guide how you react when confronted by something unexpected. Respond in a way that is in the long-term interests of the project and team relationships rather than just 'getting something off your chest'.

"Self-trust is the first secret of success"

Ralph Waldo Emerson, American essayist

 Treat 'failure' as feedback. In every project there will be times when things don't go according to plan, or even fail spectacularly! Such moments may be awkward but they needn't spell disaster. Pick up the pieces, and be honest about what has happened. What have you learned from the experience? What could be done better next time? At an appropriate distance, you may find you and your team smiling at the incident. "Wow, that was something we won't do again in a hurry!"

 Keep a work/life balance. Although passion and commitment are admirable traits in a project manager, no-one will thank you if you become a 'projectaholic', unable to focus on anything else. Look after your health and important relationships, and you will be in the best position to ensure that these outlast the project.

Avoid unnecessary heroics. Being in early may inspire your team to follow in your footsteps, but if you work 16-hour days on a regular basis, you may just demoralize them by setting unattainably high standards. You should also save your energy in case a genuine crisis occurs, and you need to work evenings and/or weekends at short notice.

Always remember that you are a role model for the project team.

Turn your plan into reality

Think of your project as a ship on an ocean-going voyage: changes in the wind and weather can mean course corrections are necessary, often at short notice. To spot these changing conditions and react quickly and decisively demands a skilled, well-led team and robust processes. It is the project manager's job to adapt the plan to reality, keeping team members focused on the task and helping them to solve problems.

6.1

Plan for change

As the singer David Bowie once said, "nothing is permanent except change". Although the nature of change is unpredictable, its occurrence on projects is almost certain.

Unplanned changes or variations include:

■ **Cost overruns.** When an activity costs more than anticipated.
■ **Schedule slippage.** When an activity takes longer than predicted, which may also lead to a cost overrun. (Whereas early finishes are rarely a cause for concern, unless there are quality implications.)
■ **Work packages delivered below quality specification.** When this happens there is often an effect on the budget and/or schedule.

case study Ben works for a financial services company and was asked to lead a three-month project to introduce real-time market information to a client's website, for a budget of $50,000. This work was quite technical but involved little change to the design of the site. During the project, the client asked if the site could be redesigned at the same time – this work was

"The best-laid schemes of mice and men go oft awry"

Robert Burns, Scottish poet

If a quality issue can't be resolved, the project's aims and baseline may need to be revised. If an unplanned cost or schedule variation occurs, try to deal with this by using the contingency (discussed in Chapter 3) you have hopefully set aside! This will avoid unnecessary, and possibly awkward, conversations with your project sponsor.

Incremental changes to a project (whether planned or unplanned) are known as *scope creep*. Types of scope creep include:

■ Tasks omitted from the original work breakdown structure.
■ Tasks where the schedule or cost have been under-estimated.
■ A decision to change the way a task will be undertaken (as a result of experience, or a shortage of resources).
■ A change of scope initiated by the project sponsor or board.

If a quality issue can't be resolved, the project's aims may need to be revised.

estimated to cost around $20,000, and would add around a month to the project duration. Ben redrew the schedule to show how the new tasks would be fitted in and their effect on the overall duration, and amended the project budget. Importantly, he also unfroze and redrew the project cost baseline, to reflect the revised scope.

6.2

Create an open culture

In order to make the right decisions in response to changing circumstances, project leaders need reliable information, a constructive approach to problem-solving, and robust procedures for authorizing forward progress. Yet it is also important not to tie a project up in 'red tape', or discourage the reporting of any deviation from the project plan.

Consider the following as key features of your change management process:

■ **Manage by exception.** Ask your team to inform you at team meetings or in weekly project reports only about things that aren't going according to plan or issues that highlight a potential future problem. Via these exception reports, you can focus attention on things that need fixing.
■ **Cultivate an 'open and fair culture'.** Encourage honest discussion and a constructive approach to problem-solving. 'Shooting the messenger' is only likely to lead to a demoralized and disconnected project team. This is particularly important with projects in areas like healthcare and aviation, where there may be safety issues at stake.

one minute wonder A key part of your project records should be a change history. This documents all the agreed changes to your project plan. As well as justifying any amendments to the project baseline, it is a useful way of highlighting trends (if, for example, a certain programming task always runs late or if deliveries from a certain supplier regularly incur extra costs).

An open and fair process of problem-solving involves three steps: to report problems as they arise; analyse their cause and effects; and review processes and suggest future improvements.

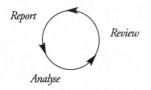

Report

Review

Analyse

Variances need to be noted and their causes discussed. If their scope falls outside of the agreed tolerance or you have insufficient contingency left to complete the project, you will need to obtain authorization to proceed from the project board or sponsor.

Regardless of whether or not you need official sanction for any changes to the project plan, it is helpful to keep your project sponsor informed: this helps build an atmosphere of trust. The 'no surprises' rule should work both ways!

Keep reporting problems, analysing causes and reviewing processes throughout your project.

Get results from team meetings

Implementing a project demands good processes, but it is people that make processes happen. You need effective ways to report and discuss progress, solve problems and make decisions.

Good project team communication can be summed up by the acronym PETS:

P = Proportionate. It is scaled to the size of the project.
E = Effective. It achieves its stated purpose.
T = Targeted. It looks at the most important issues.
S = Solutions-focused. It is positive and forward-looking.

Using one of the online collaboration tools mentioned at the back of this book is an easy, cost-effective way of keeping in touch with a team spread across sites. However, there is no substitute for face-to-face meetings. Here are some golden rules for planning meetings:

■ **Restrict the number of attendees.** Anything above seven people, and your meeting is likely to become more of a presentation. Invite only relevant attendees.

"I have left orders to be awakened at any time in case of national emergency, even if I'm in a cabinet meeting" **Former US President Ronald Reagan**

■ **Publish clear objectives.** Circulate a meeting agenda in advance.
■ **Prepare the venue.** Make sure the necessary furniture, IT equipment and pens and pencils are in place.
■ **Rehearse.** Make sure you know what you are going to say and when, and prepare for any awkward questions that might arise.

Once you've got everyone assembled, make sure you get the most out of the meeting by ensuring:

■ **Punctuality.** Start and finish on time.
■ **Confidentiality.** Allow everyone to bring problems and issues to the table, confident that these won't be discussed outside.
■ **Respect.** Allow everyone to have their say.
■ **No nitpicking.** Encourage a focus on the positive aspects of people's contributions; remember the discussion is intended to be constructive.
■ **Keep focused.** Balance staying on the agenda with allowing important and interesting ideas to surface.

Structure discussion of each point in three phases:

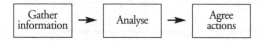

This will stop people wandering off the point, or starting to propose solutions before all the facts have been gathered and discussed.

Make sure your team meetings are relevant for all the people you invite.

6.4

Get the data

At the heart of successful project management is good decision-making – reacting appropriately to situations as they arise. To do this you need to 'get the data', as Robert McNamara, ex-President of Ford, once said.

Collating information from a variety of sources, such as stakeholder surveys and project team reports, will enable you to see the project as a system rather than a collection of work packages. From this perspective you can take decisions that are in the overall interests of the project rather than the short-term needs of one stakeholder group.

Management by walkabout is the opposite approach. It is about going on to the 'shop floor' to gain first-hand experience of how things are being done and how people are working together. Management by walkabout supplements the 'raw' data obtained from project reports, helping you to understand the 'why' behind the 'what'.

> **case study** Joy was managing a project to implement a new online purchasing system within her company. Exception reports showed that training sessions were not going to plan and continually being rescheduled and repeated. Trainees complained that the training company was adopting a one-size-fits-all approach,

■ **The OODA Loop.** The process of monitoring and controlling a project involves looking at the forces affecting the project, attempting to understand the causes and responding appropriately. One approach increasingly used in projects is known as the OODA Loop.

>**O = Observe.** What is happening that may affect the project now or in the future?
>**O = Orient.** How should the project's orientation in the wider environment affect your decisions?
>**D = Decide.** What conclusions does this lead to?
>**A = Act.** How will you turn your decisions into action?

As the name suggests, the OODA Loop is a continuous cycle. It is especially useful during a project's implementation phase.

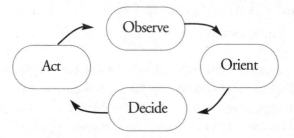

Track progress, analyse and discuss information, and react decisively.

rather than tailoring sessions to fit their needs. She also found that some staff were also training on a new intranet. She spoke with the training company, which agreed to customize its training package, and she agreed with the intranet project manager to coordinate future training to minimize 'training overload'.

6.5

Create a balanced project scorecard

Gathering all the information on project progress is important, but how do you make sense of all this data and prioritize areas for action? One method of doing this is known as a 'balanced scorecard'.

A balanced scorecard is like a driver's dashboard; it gathers together all the project performance information in one place – ideal for team meetings, or discussions with the project commissioner or project board. There are three steps in creating a balanced project scorecard:

1 At the planning stage, identify the most important indicators of project performance and how you are going to measure these. These success factors are likely to include a comparison of actual

> **case study** Patrick was leading a project to shut down a small factory, as part of a move to consolidate production within his manufacturing company. He was concerned that, although he had accurate information on progress, he was unable to get the project board to focus on the most important issues during their weekly

and projected costs; a comparison of actual and scheduled durations for completed tasks; and quality reports. For larger projects, these indicators can apply to work areas, creating a number of indicators of each type; for smaller projects, they can apply to the project as a whole.

2 Work out what constitutes moderate and severe under-performance in each case. This will enable you to identify how to present each indicator, and whether to flag it for action.

3 Highlight performance using a 'traffic light' system. For example, if a 5% variation in costs is acceptable (as it's covered by the contingency budget): a cost overrun of 2% (or any underspending) would be flagged as green (OK); an overspend of 7% would be flagged as amber (posing moderate risk to the project and requiring attention); an overspend of 12% would be flagged as red (posing severe risk to the project and requiring urgent attention). If desired, use blue to flag tasks as complete.

A balanced scorecard is a concise way of presenting information and flagging where action is most required.

round-up meetings. He put together a balanced scorecard, grouping together all the essential progress indicators, which he circulated before the meeting. This enabled him to argue persuasively for more resources to manage the staff consultation, which was in danger of running late.

6.6

There's a solution to every problem

There are two other approaches you can utilize when faced with problems: the 'five whys' method and the 'fishbone' diagram.

■ **The 'five whys' method.** This method likens a problem to an onion in that it is multi-layered – there may be underlying causes that a single question "Why did this occur?" cannot reveal. So you ask "Why?" five times (or thereabouts) as you work through layers of underlying causes. The power of 'five whys' is strikingly illustrated by an example adapted from Valerie Iles and Kim Sutherland's *Organisational Change*, where a lapse in patient care could be traced back to a decision about the organization's core strategy: Bedpan not received by patient.

case study Dave was managing a project to produce a DVD for an independent film company. The menu interface was not working as intended so he sat down with his team and asked them why. Various different answers were proposed: that the designers lacked the necessary skills, that they hadn't been briefed properly, that more rigorous testing would have meant

(Why?) →Nurse not informed. *(Why?)* →Poor handover procedures. *(Why?)* →Handover not included in induction. *(Why?)* →Training budget cut. *(Why?)* →Targets based on clinical outcomes not patient experience.

■ **A fishbone or Ishikawa diagram.** This type of diagram allows you to see how various factors may have contributed to a particular problem. In contrast to 'five whys', which can be used for problems believed to be multi-*layered*, you can use 'fishbone' to diagnose problems suspected as being multi-*faceted*. Different causes of a problem are placed as 'fishbones' along a spine leading to the appearance of a problem. (It is also possible to place smaller 'bones' along these, to show subsidiary causes.) Discussion can then focus on the relative importance of these factors, and how they have interacted to cause a problem.

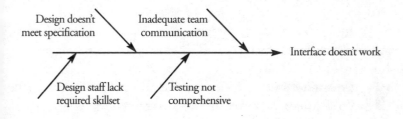

Use these methods to help sort out problems that arise.

the problem could have been resolved earlier, and so on. During the discussion it became clear that no single factor was sufficient to cause the problem, yet their cumulative effect meant that the menu did not work. Dave prioritized these causes, and discussed potential solutions with his team, before agreeing an action plan.

Be lucky!

With careful planning and preparation, you try to minimize the impact of possible bad luck on your project. But what about the positive role of chance – is there any way of increasing your 'lucky breaks'?

In *The Luck Factor*, psychology professor Richard Wiseman describes four principles that can be used to create 'luck'.

1 **Be open-minded.** Widen your field of vision to include all the possible options, rather than just the most obvious.

2 **Listen to your intuition.** It has been proven that we process information on more than one level (for example, 'sleeping on an issue' can be remarkably effective). If logic or procedure dictates

---

case study I once watched Richard Wiseman presenting to an audience of senior executives on the subject of luck and spotting business opportunities. He divided the audience into men and women, and announced he was going to show a video clip of a basketball game. He asked us to concentrate carefully, and to count the number of times the basketball changed

---

"Luck is what happens when preparation meets opportunity"

Seneca, Ancient Roman philosopher

doing one thing but instinct suggests another, take time out to reflect on why this is and whether it warrants a change of course.

 Be optimistic. If you believe in a positive outcome for your project, you will be more likely to take steps to achieve your goal.

 Turn bad luck into good. From time to time during your project things will go wrong. React to these reverses as signs of good luck ('it could have been worse' or 'that's useful to know').

There is a fifth principle that I think is worth adding: **seek out people who will help you with your project.** Build a network of people – other project managers, work colleagues and friends – that you can call on for advice. Establishing a formal mentoring relationship with a more experienced project manager can also be useful (Secret 7.7).

Good luck comes to those with the ability to look for, and find it.

hands. Following the video he asked for a show of hands: "Who thought the ball changed hands less than 12 times?" "Who thought more than 12 times?" Declining to say whether the women or men had won the count, he asked instead: "Who noticed that halfway through the film a person in a bear suit moonwalked across the basketball court?"

Maximize project learning

As the implementation stage of a project draws to a close, it is time to move into the final stage and measure its impact. Closure and evaluation are relatively neglected areas of project management. Having well-planned processes for closing a project and conducting an evaluation are vital.

7.1

Know when it's closing time

Every project has a beginning, a middle and an end. Recognizing the end of a project will sometimes be easy (a store opening event, for example), but even then there will be loose ends to tie up.

The end points for some projects – software development, for example – are often part of a recurring cycle. The closing stages of these need to be more carefully defined to avoid blurring the boundaries between projects and broader work streams.

With any project, there are tolerance levels relating to time, cost and quality (discussed in Chapter 3), where you will need authority to proceed to the next stage. If these are exceeded, a decision may be made to close the project. Your project plan should incorporate these decision points as part of the overall approach to project control.

Be prepared to close a project prior to commencement if you cannot answer satisfactorily the following questions:

■ **Aspire stage.** Are the broad project aims realistic and SMART? (See Secret 3.1.) Is the project likely to deliver tangible benefits, to our customers and the organization? Is the work required to deliver to the project within our capability (available resources) and competence (skills)?

■ Plan stage. Can quality standards be met? Is the delivery deadline achievable? Is the return on investment acceptable? Are all the people needed to deliver the project available when required? Have major risks been identified, and is the action taken to reduce their impact sufficient?

Once a the project is underway (at *Implementation* stage), consider closing the project if:

■ Cost tolerance limits have been exceeded. The project has run out of money.
■ Running too late. The project has run out of time.
■ Quality specifications cannot be met. It cannot deliver what it set out to do.
■ Organizational plans change. The project no longer fits wider business objectives.
■ The market context changes. The project is no longer feasible or appropriate.

Hopefully, of course, your project will pass all these tests and move through to planned closure at the Measure stage; this is discussed in the next Secret.

As mentioned in Chapter 2, identifying early on in the life cycle that a project is not viable should be thought of as a success rather than a failure. As well as the considerable amounts of time and money that you are likely to save by early closure, there is the benefit – harder to measure but no less real – of retaining energy and enthusiasm within your organization for the projects that will really make an impact. From your own perspective, learning to separate project winners from losers can only enhance your reputation as a project manager.

Be prepared to close a project early if it can't meet its key objectives.

7.2

Achieve closure

If all goes well, you will arrive at the point when your project has achieved its objectives. At this point, ask three questions: Have the project aims been achieved? Are stakeholders or customers satisfied? Are any necessary maintenance arrangements in place?

If you are able to answer 'yes' to all three, you can hand over and close the project. These are two elements of the 'Measure' phase of a project. The third element, evaluation, is covered in the next four Secrets.

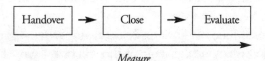

Measure

There are four essential steps to project handover and closure:

1 **Hand over the project to customers/users.** Depending on the nature of the project contract, you may need to supply ongoing support or maintenance, or training in how to use a new product or system. This is common in IT and some types of construction projects, for example. If the project is of the 'turnkey' type, you can, in theory, hand it over to the user or customer. In practice, however, there are likely to be 'post-operational' or 'snagging' issues, which you may feel should be dealt with, if only for the sake of good customer/user relationships. (For more on project contracts, see Section 4.5.)

2 **Cut off costs and finalize the budget.** Before you can compare the actual costs against estimates, you will need to finalize expenditure and formally close the project budget. If necessary, supply your accounts department with a list of project budget codes and ask them to stop accepting invoices against these. This will prevent anyone who might be tempted from posting an invoice against your project budget!

3 **Disband the project team.** At the end of the project, all the members of your project team will go their separate ways. It is important for all concerned to mark this transition. Celebrate your team's achievements! This is a good time to commemorate with a party or a meal. Thank each team member for their work, and highlight any particular personal contributions. Remind team members of any new skills gained, and opportunties to use their experience on the project in future.

4 **Identify follow-up work required.** During the project, has the need for further work arisen that is outside of the current scope? Sometimes these issues can be raised in the project evaluation, but if the issues are urgent (regarding safety, for example), or there has been a direct request from the customer or project commissioner for further work, this should be logged for immediate action.

The 'Measure' phase of a project includes these handover and closing steps.

7.3

Plan to evaluate

The final step should be to complete a project evaluation, otherwise known as a 'lessons learned' or 'impact study' report. This uses information gathered during your project to form a complete picture that highlights the successes and any failures along the way, together with the lessons learned.

Here are some of the key things to consider for an evaluation:

■ **Think about evaluation before the project even begins.** The first step in evaluation should occur at the planning stage. As well as highlighting the key success factors that your project will be measured against, the project plan should say how you will measure progress against these key success factors during and after your project.

■ **Present it in an accessible way.** A good evaluation report should clearly show all the essential information on project performance.

■ **Know your audience.** Consider your document from the reader's point of view. It is no use gathering detailed information into a 'doormat'-sized volume if the people who you will be presenting it to will just flick through the executive summary.

one minute wonder When writing your project plan, write down the project's objectives and list these in order of importance. Then ask yourself, what is the best measure of success in each of these areas, and how will I gather that information? For an example of using this approach to monitor project progress, see the North Pole Expedition case study in Secret 3.1.

■ **Be flexible about formats.** This relates to the previous point. Will the audience respond better to a verbal presentation or a written report? Do they want detailed information (to prove you have done your homework) or just the headlines?

■ **Consider past, present and future.** A good project evaluation summarizes the essential points from the completed project, is presented in a way that is relevant to its current audience, and provides information that will be useful to future project managers.

■ **Focus on the process as well the outcomes.** "What have we learned to do?" is just as important a question as "What have we done?"

When planning an evaluation, you will need to determine the purpose and scope (range) of your evaluation, and how you will gather the information. The next Secret helps you identify what to measure.

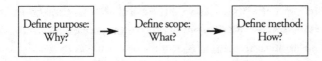

Define purpose: Why? → Define scope: What? → Define method: How?

Evaluation should start early in a project, and be written up or presented during the final 'Measure' phase.

7.4

Choose what to measure

There are various levels on which an evaluation works. For the project manager, commissioner and stakeholders, it provides a summary of the project's accomplishments. For the organization as a whole, it is an indicator of the project's wider implications.

In *The Project Management Scorecard* (see further reading), Jack Phillips describes five levels at which a project manager should aim to conduct an evaluation:

1 **Stakeholder satisfaction.** Measures of customer and stake-holder perception describe the effect of your project on others. For example: '80 per cent of our customers found the new online ordering system easier to use'.

case study Following an organizational merger, Cathy compiled an evaluation report that included the following headlines: 95% of staff had a 'good' understanding of the new company structure; 75% of

2 **Skills and knowledge gained.** By definition, a project involves doing something new, so it is not surprising that project working can require a fresh approach, or that unexpected problems may arise. Especially in today's world of rapid technological change, new skills and knowledge are an important part of the overall benefits a project can provide.

3 **Implementation and application.** By citing examples of where teams and individuals have done things faster, more creatively or more efficiently, you will be providing a pointer for future projects on how they can apply new working methods.

4 **Business impact.** A key measure of a project's success is its commercial results. Alongside 'hard' monetary data such as cost and income information, you can include 'soft' data, such as customer satisfaction, innovation and successful task completion, project team training, qualifications and performance.

5 **Return on investment (ROI).** While raw financial information offers an important view of project performance, the picture it provides can be rather superficial. The true return on investment can only be ascertained by comparing the likely gains to the organization from the various types of impact described above, against the overall costs.

Measure only those elements that are relevant for the audience.

project tasks had been completed on time; three potential 'process innovations' (new working methods) had been identified; the project had spent 97% of its allocated budget.

7.5

Measure the true return on investment

As mentioned in the previous Secret, calculating the long-term contribution of a project involves combining 'hard' and 'soft' data to make predictions about the future. This is a bit like trying to compare grapes and wine – the grapes may look very nice, but how many bottles of wine will they produce?

So, what is the best way to compare the immediate benefits of the project with longer-term benefits like new knowledge and improved processes? Consider the following issues:

■ **What processes are in place for translating knowledge into practice?** Are there regular staff appraisals, a flexible management open to new ideas, and people willing to champion change?
■ **How good is the 'organizational memory'?** Is there an induction process for new team members, exit interviews, and a regularly updated procedures manual?
■ **What is the organization's track record in implementing change?** Are new initiatives generally embraced enthusiastically, or do they often fall by the wayside after encountering resistance?

> "The three most important things you need to measure in business are customer satisfaction, employee satisfaction and cash flow" **Jack Welch, Lessons for Success**

Another question worth asking is how you can translate 'soft' data (customer and staff attitudes and satisfaction rates, for example) into financial information. Consider these two points:

■ Expressing measures of attitudes and perception in a single 'currency' of business impact – usually a financial one – is not always easy. Often, it involves comparing the projects with other similar ones either inside or outside the company. When it can be done, however, the effort will often be worthwhile.

■ The amount of information you provide should suit the size of the project, and the requirements of the various stakeholders. Valuable though attempting to measure the future impact of your project is, there may be times when the best use of project resources, and of your time as a project manager, is to avoid such sophisticated attempts at impact measurement. You can then rely on a mixture of easily obtainable project cost information and a list of more immediate benefits.

To assess long-term impact, you will need to look beyond the project into the wider organization.

7.6

Evaluation is a listening exercise

When compiling a project evaluation, you will need to combine good observation and memory of the project with a number of more formal methods of gathering information. These include:

■ **Project performance information.** This is why you spent all that time preparing a project plan and gathering progress information throughout the project! Gather together your Gantt charts for schedule performance, the project budget for cost performance, team meeting notes, exception reports and change history documents.

■ **Surveys and questionnaires.** This type of written feedback is very useful if you want to gather information from a large number of people – though you will often need to enourage people to fill them in! Surveys

> **case study** Following a major annual conference, Louise organized a focus group of delegates to obtain their views about the conference. She then sought the views of senior management, sharing with them information about income from delegate fees and

are a relatively quick way of obtaining stakeholders' views. They are best suited to multiple-choice questioning, which may mean that the information you receive is rather superficial.

■ **Interviews and focus groups.** These are more time-consuming, but often reveal information not included in surveys. They are a chance to talk to the project's stakeholders, often in a more informal setting, to gather their views about the project: how it met their objectives, what they believe worked well, and suggested areas for future improvement. Interviews and focus groups can often add a useful layer of 'why' to the 'what' expressed through surveys and questionnaires.

Just as an evaluation report needs to be tailored to its intended audience (as discussed earlier in this chapter), it is important to include the right people in any interviews and surveys. Include those stakeholders most affected by the project, and who have the most influence over future projects. Divide the stakeholders into groups, including the three main ones – commissioner, customers/users and suppliers – and ask each group questions relevant to their objectives and involvement in the project.

Gather the necessary data and ask the different groups of stakeholders for feedback.

sponsorship. Lastly, she asked the major suppliers for feedback. Louise then combined all these views into a comprehensive evaluation document, which included a list of the project's achievements and suggestions for how next year's conference could be improved.

7.7

Never stop learning

Now you've read this book, you are familiar with some of the tools and techniques used by today's project managers, and you know how and where to apply them. As your career in project management progresses, you can look forward to increasing your knowledge and experience further.

After 20 years in project management, I have acquired a reasonable amount of knowledge, but am constantly reminded what a broad discipline it is, and how much there still is to discover. Here are some ways you can continue your professional development:

■ **Read widely.** The list of further reading at the back of this book is just a small selection of the wide body of knowledge on project management. Beyond this, read up on any subject that interests you, from the business news, to books on leadership, to corporate strategy. You are bound to come across many links with project management!

■ **Join a professional body.** The UK Association for Project Management (APM) and the US-based Project Management Institute (PMI) both offer various grades of membership, to suit all stages of professional development. Membership entitles you to free and

"Only those who dare to fail greatly can ever achieve greatly"

Robert F. Kennedy, US senator

reduced-cost training courses and publications, as well as access to meetings and professional networks.

■ **Take a training course.** There are a wide range of training courses available. These range from short courses aimed at covering the basics in a day or two, to degree courses at undergraduate and masters levels. In between are courses that provide a qualification in a recognized project approach (such as PRINCE2™).

■ **Find a mentor.** There is often no substitute for having a guide through the jungle of project management. A good mentor will be able to use his or her experience to help you make important decisions, and boost your confidence in handling potentially difficult situations. While a coach will aim to help you make the most of your existing skills and experience, a mentor will actually have 'been there before', so can add their wisdom to your own.

■ **Stay positive.** A well-known phrase in leadership coaching is that there is 'no failure, only feedback'. While in project management you will not achieve unqualified succcess every time, good project managers are able to treat these temporary reverses as learning experiences, and to reflect on them as part of a quest to continually refine and improve their approach.

Keep on learning, and good luck in your project management career!

Jargon buster

Actual cost
The incurred costs that are charged to the project budget and for which payment has been made, or accrued.

'Agile'
The breaking down of work into small units, with minimal long-term planning.

Approach
A series of techniques grouped together to form an overall method.

Baseline schedule
The fixed project schedule. It is the standard by which the project schedule performance is measured.

Budgeted cost
The cost anticipated at the start of a project.

Cashflow
The process of payment and receipt of funds to and from the project budget.

Competitive tender
A formal procurement process whereby contractors are given an equal chance to tender for the supply of goods or services.

Contingency
The planned allotment of time and cost or other resources for the unforseeable risks within a project. Something held in reserve.

Contract cost basis
The way in which supplier contracts are constructed.

Contract scope
The extent of the work a supplier is asked to undertake.

Cost variance
The difference between the planned and actual expenditure.

Critical path
The route through activities on the plan. Delays to the critical path delay the project end date.

Effort-driven task
A task where the time taken to complete it reduces in proportion to the number of people working on it.

Lag time
The minimum necessary lapse of time between the finish of one activity and the finish of an overlapping activity. The delay incurred between two specified activities.

Network diagram
A visual presentation of project data in which the logical order of tasks determines the placement of the activities.

PRINCE2™
Projects In Controlled Environments. A framework for developing projects.

Procurement
The process of obtaining goods and services from suppliers.

Project board
A group, usually comprising of the sponsor, senior managers and sometimes key stake-holders, whose job it is to set the strategic direction of a project. It gives guidance to the project manager and the sponsor.

Project brief or mandate
An initial project document, later clarified by the project plan.

Project plan
Builds on the project brief, to provide a complete picture of how the project will be managed.

Resources
All those elements that are required to undertake a project. Resources can include people, finance and materials.

Risk assessment
A structured process that allows risks to be managed proactively by minimizing threats and maximizing opportunities.

Schedule slippage
The excess time required to complete the project over and above that planned.

Scope creep
These are planned (or unplanned) changes to a project. It is important to amend the project's baseline costs and schedule, as the final (actual) outcomes should now be measured against those new targets.

Slack
The amount of time that an activity may be delayed from its start without delaying the project finish date.

Sponsor
The person who asks a project manager to undertake the project, and to whom he or she is accountable for its success.

Stakeholder
Any person or organization with an interest in the outcome of your project.

Supplier
An external company that will undertake the design and delivery of a product or service.

Task information
All the important information relating to a task, including duration, cost and resources required.

Turnkey
A type of contract in which the product or service is built, tested and delivered into the client's care.

WBS
Work Breakdown Structure. The hierarchical structure of project tasks.

Work package
A related group of tasks.

Further reading

Project management and business strategy

Association of Project Management *Project Risk Analysis and Management Guide* (APM Publishing, 2004) ISBN 978-1-903494-1-7

Association of Project Management *Project Management Body of Knowledge* (APM Publishing, 5th edn 2006) ISBN 978-1-903494-13-4

Laufer, A. and Hoffman, E.J. *Project Management Success Stories* (John Wiley, 2000) ISBN 978-0471360070

Levine, H. *Practical Project Management – Tips, Tactics and Tools* (John Wiley, 2002) ISBN 978-0471203032

Maylor, H. *Project Management* (Pearson, 1999) ISBN 978-0273704317

Nokes, S. and Kelly, S. *The Definitive Guide to Project Management* (FT Press, 2008) ISBN 978-0273710974

O'Connell, F. *Simply Brilliant: The competitive Advantage of Common Sense* (Pearson) ISBN 978-0273720775

Phillips, J.J., Bothell, T.W. and Snead, G.L. *The Project Management Scorecard: Measuring the Success of Project Management Solutions* (Butterworth-Heinemann, 2002) ISBN 978-0750674492

Reiss, G. *Project Management Demystified* (Taylor & Francis, 2007) ISBN 978-0415421638

Sun Tzu *The Art of War* (Shambala, 1991 edn) ISBN 978-1599869773

Team leadership and communication

Belbin, R.M. *Management Teams: Why They Succeed or Fail* (Butterworth-Heinemann, 2010) ISBN 978-1856178075

Briner, W., Geddes, M. and Hastings, C. *Project Leadership* (Gower, 1990) ISBN 978-0-566-07785-2

Charvet, S.R. *Words that Change Minds: Mastering the Language of Influence* (Kendall/Hunt, 1995) ISBN 978-0787234799

Covey, Stephen R. *7 Habits of Highly Effective People: Powerful Lessons in Personal Change* (Simon and Schuster, 2004) ISBN 978-0743272452

Marlier, D., Parker, C. and Mobilizing Teams International *Engaging Leadership – Three Agendas for Sustaining Achievement* (Palgrave Macmillan, 2009) ISBN 978-0230577527

Morrell, M. and Capparell, S. *Shackleton's Way* (Nicholas Brealey, 2001) ISBN 978-1857882117

Wiseman, R. *The Luck Factor* (Arrow, 2004) ISBN 978-1401359416

Selected online resources/project software

Basecamp:
Collaboration tool that allows you to manage small and medium-sized projects online.
www.basecamphq.com

Copper:
Popular and comprehensive online resource, with several different subscription options available. US-based.
www.copperproject.com

Merlin and Project X:
Medium-sized project planning tools for Mac OS (as opposed to Windows) users.
www.projectx.com
www.projectwizards.net

Microsoft (MS) Project:
A widely used planning, scheduling and estimating tool. Comes into its own for larger projects, with an 'enterprise'-level version that enables multi-site working.
http://office.microsoft.com/en-us/project/default.aspx

Milestone Simplicity:
Scheduling software that integrates with Microsoft programs
www.kidasa.com/Simplicity

Primavera SureTrak:
The 'little brother' of the Primavera family of project management software.
www.oracle.com/applications/primavera/primavera-suretrak.html

Project in a Box:
Software and services for project managers from single users through to corporations.
www.projectinabox.org.uk

Projectplace:
A comprehensive online project management tool, with either free single-user or paid multi-user licences available. Based in Europe, and translated into several different languages.
www.projectplace.com

TurboProject:
Rather more comprehensive, the 'express' version is designed for smaller projects.
www.turboproject.com

Other resources

Templates for many of the forms referred to in this book are can be downloaded free from **www.matthewbatchelor.co.uk**. This site also contains details of project management courses and consultancy services offered by the author in the UK and internationally.

www.BusinessSecrets.net